Tiger Shark

by Jenna Lee Gleisner

Bullfrog Books

Ideas for Parents and Teachers

Bullfrog Books let children practice reading informational text at the earliest reading levels. Repetition, familiar words, and photo labels support early readers.

Before Reading

- Discuss the cover photo. What does it tell them?

- Look at the picture glossary together. Read and discuss the words.

Read the Book

- "Walk" through the book and look at the photos. Let the child ask questions. Point out the photo labels.

- Read the book to the child, or have him or her read independently.

After Reading

- Prompt the child to think more. Ask: Tiger sharks get their name from the patterns on their skin. Can you name other animals with notable patterns?

Bullfrog Books are published by Jump!
5357 Penn Avenue South
Minneapolis, MN 55419
www.jumplibrary.com

Library of Congress Cataloging-in-Publication Data

Names: Gleisner, Jenna Lee, author.
Title: Tiger shark / by Jenna Lee Gleisner.
Description: Bullfrog books edition.
Minneapolis, MN : Jump!, Inc., [2020]
Series: Shark bites
Includes bibliographical references and index.
Audience: Age 5-8. | Audience: K to Grade 3.
Identifiers: LCCN 2019001201 (print)
LCCN 2019002853 (ebook)
ISBN 9781641289689 (ebook)
ISBN 9781641289672 (hardcover : alk. paper)
Subjects: LCSH: Tiger shark—Juvenile literature.
Classification: LCC QL638.95.C3 (ebook)
LCC QL638.95.C3 G545 2020 (print)
DDC 597.3/4—dc23
LC record available at https://lccn.loc.gov/2019001201

Editors: Susanne Bushman and Jenna Trnka
Design: Shoreline Publishing Group

Photo Credits: Yoshinori/Shutterstock, cover, 9; Frhojdysz/Dreamstime, 1; Willtu/Dreamstime, 3; National Geographic Image Collection/Alamy, 4, 23bl; Andre Seale/Alamy, 5; Michael Bogner/Dreamstime, 6–7, 22, 23tl; Scubazoo/Alamy, 8; Tommy Schultz/Dreamstime, 10–11, 23br; Andrey Nekrasov/Alamy, 12–13, 23tr; Tatiana Belova/Shutterstock, 14; Rich Carey/Shutterstock, 15; ACEgan/Shutterstock, 16–17; Rodrigo Friscone/Getty, 18–19; Media Drum World/Alamy, 20–21; Photon75/Shutterstock, 24.

Printed in the United States of America at Corporate Graphics in North Mankato, Minnesota.

Table of Contents

Striped Shark

This shark pup is small.

It is a tiger shark!

It gets its name from its stripes.

It grows big.
The stripes fade.

Its belly is white.

But the dark color
on top helps it hunt.

How?

Prey doesn't
see it coming.

Like what?

This school
of tuna.

Good sight and smell help it find prey.

Then it attacks!

Tiger sharks will eat many things.

Like what?

Fish. Rays. Seals.

ray

14

What else? Sea snakes.

Birds.

Even old tires!

sea
snake

15

Sea turtles, too.
Sharp teeth help.
Powerful jaws, too.

What if they crack
or break a tooth?

No problem.

A new one grows
in the next day!

Time to hunt!
What will it find to eat?

Parts of a Tiger Shark

dorsal fin
This fin on top
of a shark's body
helps it balance.

tail fin
Also called the caudal
fin. This shark moves
slow, but its large tail
fin helps with bursts
of speed to catch prey.

gills
Sharks and other
fish use gills to
breathe underwater.

body
Tiger sharks can grow
to be around 18 feet
(5.5 meters) long
and 2,000 pounds
(907 kilograms).

pectoral fins
Large pectoral fins
help tiger sharks steer
while swimming.

Picture Glossary

fade
To disappear slowly or lose color.

prey
Animals that are hunted by other animals for food.

pup
A baby shark.

school
A tight group of fish that swims and feeds together.

Index

To Learn More

Finding more information is as easy as 1, 2, 3.

❶ Go to www.factsurfer.com

❷ Enter "tigershark" into the search box.

❸ Choose your book to see a list of websites.